A CHOICE OF
GEORGE HERBERT'S
VERSE

selected

with an introduction by

R. S. THOMAS

passage   commentary
           essay a A + c choice
essays   victorias
           Auden
           r Herbert

FABER AND FABER
24 Russell Square
London

First published in this edition in 1967
by Faber and Faber Limited
24 Russell Square London W.C.1
Reprinted 1969
Printed in Great Britain
by R. MacLehose and Company Limited
The University Press Glasgow
All rights reserved

S.B.N. FPCE 571 08189 4
S.B.N. Cloth 571 08110 X

A CHOICE OF
GEORGE HERBERT'S VERSE

Editor's Note

In this selection from George Herbert's verse I have chosen mainly those poems which seem to me satisfactory as such. I am grateful to Mr F. E. Hutchinson for making sense of line 21 in 'The Collar' and have adopted his placing of a fullstop after 'not' in his edition of *The Works of George Herbert* published by the Oxford University Press in 1941.

read Tieplough, pilgruage

Contents

Introduction

George Herbert was born in Montgomery castle in April 1593, and died in Bemerton, Wiltshire, at the age of forty; an early death, but not unusual in those troubled and dangerous days. He was, as we should say, well-connected, being descended on his father's side from the earls of Pembroke, and on his mother's from a family of Shropshire knights, the Newports. His mother, Magdalen Herbert, later the friend of John Donne, was a remarkable woman. It was largely owing to her efforts that both George and his elder brother Edward received that thorough grounding in letters, which later stood them in such good stead. And as for their spiritual care, Walton tells us that:

'In this time of her Widowhood, she being desirous to give Edward her eldest son such advantages of Learning and other education as might suit his birth and fortune: and thereby make him the more fit for the service of his Country: did at his being of a fit age remove from Montgomery Castle with him, and some of her younger sons to Oxford; and having entered Edward into Queens College, and provided him a fit Tutor, she commended him to his care; yet she continued there with him, and still kept him in a moderate awe of herself: and so much under her own eye, as to see and converse with him daily; but she managed this power over him without any such rigid sourness, as might make her company a torment to her Child; but with such a sweetness and complyance with the recreations and pleasures of youth, as did incline him willingly to spend much of his time in the company of his dear and careful Mother.'

And although George himself went to Cambridge at the age of fifteen, he is unlikely to have escaped so benevolent an influence.

George Herbert graduated at Trinity College at the age of eighteen, and became a fellow of his college when he was twenty-two. A further honour came to him in 1619, when he was made Orator for the University, a position which brought him to the notice of the King. According to Walton he had by now 'acquir'd great Learning, and was blest with a high fancy, a civil and sharp wit, and with a natural elegance, both in his behaviour, his tongue and his pen.'

Herbert continued as Orator for eight years, in great hopes of advancement to higher position, for had not both his predecessors become secretaries of State? However, his prospects were considerably impaired, first by the death of his two most influential friends, and later by that of King James himself. Walton sees the finger of God in this. It is certainly intriguing to conjecture what would have become of Herbert the poet had he gained preferment at Court, instead of being diverted into Holy Orders to become a pattern of virtue to all other wearers of the cloth.

He now withdrew to the residence of a friend in Kent, where in solitude and retirement he turned over in his mind the differing claims of Court and Church, resolving finally to proceed to the taking of Holy Orders, which he must have done somewhere around 1626, for in July of that year he was made Prebend of Layton Ecclesia in Lincoln Diocese. In 1629 he fell ill, and went to live with his brother in Essex for a year, curing himself by living on a diet of his own making. He was not of a strong constitution, and sickness was never to be far away. This may partly account for the frequent mention of illness in his poetry, although that never reaches morbidity. In fact Herbert like a good Anglican equates sickness with sin, and good health with holiness, believing implicitly in God's power to heal, if it be also his will. And in one of his sections in 'A Priest to the Temple' he stresses a knowledge of medicaments as being indispensable to a cure of souls.

Feeling now considerably better, Herbert determined both to marry and to take priest's orders. His betrothal to Jane Danvers is quaintly and movingly described by Walton. 'This Mr Danvers having known him long, and familiarly, did so much affect him, that he often and publickly declar'd a desire that Mr Herbert would marry any of his Nine Daughters, but rather his Daughter Jane, because Jane was his beloved Daughter: And he had often said the same to Mr Herbert himself; and that if he could like her for a Wife, and she him for a Husband, Jane should have a double blessing: and Mr Danvers had so often said the like to Jane, and

8

so much commended Mr Herbert to her, that Jane became so much a Platonick, as to fall in love with Mr Herbert unseen.'

George Herbert's ordination to the priesthood brought him, after much praying and searching of heart, to the parish of Bemerton, which was to be the scene both of that rare pastoral care, reflected in 'A Priest to the Temple' and also of that even rarer product, the poetry of 'The Temple'. At Bemerton Herbert both greatly endeared himself to his parishioners, and also gently but firmly led them, persuading the large majority to join him in saying the Daily Office at ten and at four o'clock. To quote Walton once more: 'Thus he continued meditating and praying and rejoicing till the day of his death'.

The Elizabethan age was well advanced by the time Herbert was born. The danger from Spain was over. The Elizabethan settlement had had a chance to consolidate itself. But it was an age of adventure and pioneering as well as of achievement. It is characteristic of a great epoch to produce great men in many different walks of life. At this time there were striking figures at Court and in the Church, and not least in literature. It is perhaps seldom remembered that George Herbert was a younger contemporary of Shakespeare. Side by side with the growing vitality of the English people, there was the English language, expanding and developing in suppleness and range. And as the embodiment of that people at worship there was the Anglican Church, shaped by the Prayer Book with its sonorous yet balanced cadences, and patronised first by Elizabeth and then by James I. The greatest achievement of this church perhaps was to match the breadth and vigour of the age with the richness and freshness of its versions of the Bible and Prayer Book. Anglicanism represents the recovery of nerve after the loss of it by the mediaeval Church, and was a product of the English mind at a seminal stage in its development. And the emphasis is on mind, for the appeal of Anglicanism was to the intellect via the language, as witness the case of John Donne. And yet, while emphasising the intellectual content of Anglicanism, we must not forget that its best exponents, Lancelot Andrewes, Nicholas Ferrar, Alice Thornton and George Herbert himself, were just as devout and punctilious as the best of the Puritans, and possibly a good deal warmer.

9

It was into such a Church that Herbert was born, and in it he grew up, guided at first by his mother and the wise chaplains she procured for him, and later by its very attraction and congeniality to his own sweet yet disciplined nature:

> 'I joy, deare Mother, when I view
> Thy perfect lineaments, and hue
> > Both sweet and bright.
>
> Beauty in thee takes up her place,
> And dates her letters from thy face,
> > When she doth write.'

It is a commonplace about Anglicanism that it was an attempt to steer a middle course between two extremes, avoiding the excesses of the Romans on the one hand and of the Puritans on the other. It aimed to restore and preserve all that was sound and right, and to celebrate it in the balanced and beautiful prose of the period. The appeal of this movement to Herbert is evident in his poetry. What briefer and better description is there of the ideals of the Anglican Church than this line of his from the 'British Church' quoted above?

> 'Neither too mean, nor yet too gay.'

Time and again, too, he speaks of that moderation and dignified humility, which attend the best type of Anglican:

> 'Give me the pliant minde, whose gentle measure
> > Complies and suits with all estates;
> Which can let loose to a crowne and yet with pleasure
> > Take up within a cloister's gates.'

Or again:

> 'A Christian's state and case
> Is not a corpulent but a thinne and spare
> Yet active strength: whose long and bonie face
> > Content and care
> Do seem to equally divide
> Like a pretender, not a bride.'

He can welcome Lent, not as a time of misery and mortification, but as an opportunity to be temperate:

> 'Welcome deare feast of Lent: who loves not thee,
> He loves not Temperance or Authoritie,
>   But is compos'd of passion.'

We have already seen how early Christianity was exercising its influence on Herbert:

> 'Since, Lord, to thee
> A narrow way and little gate
> Is all the passage, on my infancie
> Thou didst lay hold, and antedate
> My faith in me.'

Both at Westminster and later at Cambridge, there was nothing but praise for his engaging saintliness; and already he was acknowledging the above influence in verse. According to Walton it was at the early age of seventeen that he sent his mother the sonnet beginning:

> 'My God, where is that ancient heat towards Thee...'

with that play upon words which was so attractive to the metaphysical poets. And yet in the young Herbert there took place, though perhaps in a quieter way than in Augustine, for instance, that age-old struggle between God and the world, the spirit and the flesh, call it what you will. He came of gentle birth. The appeal of the court was natural. He had influential friends. He had been noticed by King James himself. How better explain the frequent references in his verse to clothes and odours, than as a sublimation of a once very real desire? The clothes and the bearing, the good form, which once were to have distinguished the courtier, have now been transferred to the churchman in God's presence. Hence his excellent definition of prayer as 'man well drest'. Hence also his reminder that:

> 'In clothes cheap handsomnesse doth bear the bell.
> Wisedome's a trimmer thing than shop e'er gave.'

But Herbert remained a poet as well. Let it not be thought that, in consecrating himself to God, he had put entirely on one side the delights of the senses. He has many references to scents and perfumes, as already stated. Perhaps the most strikingly sensuous is the first stanza from 'The Odour':

> 'How sweetly doth My Master sound! My Master!
>> As Amber-Grease leaves a rich sent
>>> Unto the taster:
>> So do these words a sweet content,
> An orientall fragrancie, My Master.'

Nevertheless, in that tall but delicate frame of Herbert's there was an iron resolve. Once the choice between the world and God had been made, he never faltered. All his gifts, his desires, his possessions were to be devoted to the service of the Master just mentioned. This was the transference of the courtier's allegiance. But this, too, was humility, not grovelling.

> 'Yet, though thou troublest me, I must be meek;
>> In weaknesse must be stout.
> Well, I will change the service, and go seek
>> Some other Master out.
> Ah, my deare God! though I am clean forgot,
> Let me not love thee, if I love thee not.'

Yeats said that out of his quarrel with others a man makes rhetoric, but out of his quarrel with himself poetry. Herbert surely had no quarrel with others. What he had was an argument, not with others, nor with himself primarily, but with God; and God always won. There is at times in him an element of feminine surrender, corrected at others by a more manly turning of the argument at the very moment of defeat:

> 'But thou wilt sinne and grief destroy,
> That so the broken bones may joy,
> And tune together in a well-set song,
>> Full of his praises,
>> Who dead men raises.
> Fractures well cur'd make us more strong.'

'The good die first,' Wordsworth reminds us, 'and those whose hearts are dry as summer dust burn to the socket.' It is a truism of the Christian life that the most saintly are the most conscious of sin.

This certainly was a real and constant ingredient in Herbert, causing him deeper regret than any mere weakness of body.

> 'Sorrie I am, my God, sorrie I am,
> That my offences course it in a ring.'

When I think of George Herbert, I remember how he lay prostrate on the floor of Bemerton church at his induction. Walton writes:

'When at his induction he was shut into Bemerton Church, being left there alone to Toll the Bell, he staid so much longer than an ordinary time, before he returned to those Friends expecting him at the Church door, that his Friend, Mr Woodnot looked in at the Church window, and saw him lie prostrate on the ground before the Altar; at which time and place (as he after told Mr Woodnot) he set some Rules to himself for the future manage of his life; and then and there made a vow, to labour to keep them.'

That physical prostration was but the outward sign of that contrition and humility, which possessed his heart and led him to sing of himself as, 'Lesse than the least of all God's mercies.' But, when all is said and done, this cannot be the last word on Herbert. He sings of sin and humility, and of the soul's argument with God most certainly. But that is not his main theme. His main theme is love, Christian love; the love that is in God, and the charity that attends a true Christian:

> 'King of Glorie, King of Peace,
> I will love thee;
> And that love may never cease
> I will move thee.'

Or again:

> 'Immortal love, author of this great frame,
> Sprung from that beautie which can never fade.'

Some little while ago, an unlovely predilection for endearments disfigured much English verse of the day. The word 'darling' for instance, was at a premium. If there was one poet who could have used endearments with any success, it was Herbert. For his love for God, despite its purity, was a creaturely love, and more than tinged with emotion. Yet I can recall but one example, apt and proper as that is:

> 'Love said, You shall be he.
> I the unkinde, ungrateful? Ah, my deare,
> I cannot look on thee.'

What of Herbert's metric? Poetry has been said to be the result of a metre-making argument. This is what sometimes we miss in this poet. What is present, although by no means over-indulged, is the Metaphysicals' liking for puns, conceits and over-ingeniously contrived analogies:

> 'If all men's tears were let
> Into one common sewer, sea and brine,
> What were they all compar'd to thine?
> Wherein, if they were set,
> They would discolour thy most bloudy sweat.'

And the lovely beginning of 'Vertue' with its 'sweet day, so cool, so calm, so bright', is marred for me by the miscarrying image at the end:

> 'Onely a sweet and vertuous soul,
> Like season'd timber never gives;
> But though the whole world turn to coal,
> Then chiefly lives.'

There is too often the impression that the verse is being made subordinate to an idea, and not that the idea emerges naturally from the poetry. Yet Herbert was not just a man of a fixed idea. He had great interest in music, for instance, and was himself a skilled musician, as so many in that period were. Not only are there many references to music and to musical instruments in his verse, but at times his own muse glides into a tune of beautiful simplicity:

> 'Come, my Joy, my Love, my Heart:
> Such a Joy as none can move:
> Such a Love, as none can part:
> Such a Heart, as joyes in love.'

And, indeed, the more one thinks of it, the less can Herbert be accused of metrical poverty. There is after all a great variety of verse forms deployed by him, from the moving simplicity of:

> 'I got me flowers to straw thy way;
> I got me boughs off many a tree:
> But thou wast up by break of day,
> And broughtst thy sweets along with thee,'

to the richer orchestration of 'The Collar' which begins:

> 'I struck the board, and cry'd, No more.
> I will abroad.
> What? Shall I ever sigh and pine?
> My lines and life are free, free as the rode,
> Loose as the winde, as large as store'.

As I have already indicated, Herbert was fortunate in being able to draw on the freshness and vitality of the English of his day. Like many another poet, more interested in what he had to say than in ways of saying it, he was no innovator, but took the language as he found it. Yet owing to his dates, he was able to do this with more relish than those born much later. As he says in 'The Sonne':

> 'Let forrain nations of their language boast,
> What fine varietie each tongue affords:
> I like our language, as our men and coast:
> Who cannot dresse it well, want wit not words'.

In the Book of Common Prayer also, and in the worship of the Anglican church he found many of his favourite ideas, together with the vocabulary to express them. And in his use of a word like 'secretarie' he showed himself ready and able to profit from the innovations in verse of such a man as John Donne.

There remains to ask, What is George Herbert's relevance to to-day? And this is bound up with the relevance of Christianity, and with the possibility of a fruitful relationship between Christianity and poetry. The bridge between the two latter is the Incarnation. If poetry is concerned with the concrete and the particular, then Christianity aims at their redemption and consecration. The poet invents the metaphor, and the Christian lives it. Herbert is first and foremost a Christian, but he is an Anglican, too. Is

Anglicanism still a live issue? I think he shows that it can be. In his day, it was allied to a swiftly emerging power. To-day it could still be more than something 'to shore against our ruins'. The decline of England as a major power need not mean that there are not other things to cultivate, other aims to pursue. This poet's description of prayer recurs, 'man well-drest'. He inherited the fruits of the Elizabethan Settlement, and was able to extract the poetry instead of having to argue and debate with his opponents. Could not the removal of the 'white man's burden', as it were, give the twentieth century Englishman time for other things? And one of those things, one of the main things, as Herbert demonstrates, is both the possibility and the desirability of a friendship with God. Friendship is no longer the right way to describe it. The word now is dialogue, encounter, confrontation; but the realities engaged have not altered all that much.

Another of Herbert's relevances is his commitment. To him Anglicanism was a way of life. It was the commitment to an order of reason, discipline and propriety, embodied in a Church solidly based on Scripture and the Book of Common Prayer. Is this deliberate submission to such a wholesome way of life entirely without relevance or appeal at the present time? Amid all the varied and often conflicting possibilities, which can but distract the soul or gull the mind with a false sense of freedom, there is always the part that a consciously accepted discipline can play in determining a man's attitude to life's challenge. For many to-day that discipline is equated with communism, socialism, humanism. Could it not be as well or even better Anglicanism? This is the question which Herbert still poses. But perhaps there is a difference in the climate of our thought. In him there is often the mediaevalist's depreciation of this life, with a corresponding eagerness for the next, as in 'Time' or 'Man's Medley':

> 'Yet if we rightly measure,
>   Man's joy and pleasure
> Rather hereafter, then in present is.'

But in order to refute any overriding sense of world-negation, it is necessary to quote only a line or two from such a poem as 'The Flower':

> 'How fresh, O Lord, how sweet and clean
> Are thy returns, ev'n as flowers in Spring'.

Just as a stanza from 'Discipline' can disarm criticism of Herbert as being too austere:

> 'Throw away thy rod,
> Throw away thy wrath:
>   O my God,
> Take the gentle path.'

This, then, is Herbert's relevance for to-day. He commends a way of life for the individual that is still viable. It is reason, not so much tinged with, as warmed by emotion, and solidly based on order and discipline, the soul's good form. This way of life he celebrates in verse that is sometimes quaint, sometimes over-ingenious, but never trite. It escapes prettiness, and has rather, at times, the simplicity and gravity of great poetry. It is a proof of the eternal beauty of holiness.

R. S. THOMAS

Antiphon

Cho. Let all the world in ev'ry corner sing,
         My God and King.

     Vers. The heav'ns are not too high,
              His praise may thither flie :
              The earth is not too low,
              His praises there may grow.

Cho. Let all the world in ev'ry corner sing,
         My God and King.

     Vers. The church with psalms must shout,
              No doore can keep them out :
              But above all, the heart
              Must bear the longest part.

Cho. Let all the world in ev'ry corner sing,
         My God and King.

Stanzas from *The Church-Porch*

Drink not the third glasse, which thou canst not tame,
When once it is within thee ; but before
Mayst rule it, as thou list ; and poure the shame,
Which it would poure on thee, upon the floore.
  It is most just to throw that on the ground,
   Which would throw me there, if I keep the round.

He that is drunken, may his mother kill
Bigge with his sister : he hath lost the reins,
Is outlaw'd by himself : all kinde of ill
Did with his liquour slide into his veins.
  The drunkard forfets Man, and doth devest
   All worldly right, save what he hath by beast.

Shall I, to please anothers wine-sprung minde,
Lose all mine own? God hath giv'n me a measure
Short of his canne, and bodie; must I finde
A pain in that, wherein he findes a pleasure?
   Stay at the third glasse: if thou lose thy hold,
   Then thou are modest, and the wine grows bold.

If reason move not Gallants, quit the room,
(All in a shipwrack shift their severall way)
Let not a common ruine thee intombe:
Be not a beast in courtesie; but stay,
   Stay at the third cup, or forgo the place.
   Wine above all things doth Gods stamp deface.

Yet, if thou sinne in wine or wantonnesse,
Boast not thereof; nor make thy shame thy glorie.
Frailtie gets pardon by submissivenesse;
But he that boasts, shuts that out of his storie.
   He makes flat warre with God, and doth defie
   With his poore clod of earth the spacious sky.

      *   *   *   *   *

Be thriftie, but not covetous: therefore give
Thy need, thine honour, and thy friend his due.
Never was scraper brave man. Get to live;
Then live, and use it: els, it is not true
   That thou hast gotten. Surely use alone
   Makes money not a contemptible stone.

Never exceed thy income. Youth may make
Ev'n with the yeare: but age, if it will hit,
Shoots a bow short, and lessens still his stake,
As the day lessens, and his life with it.
   Thy children, kindred, friends upon thee call;
   Before thy journey fairly part with all.

Yet in thy thriving still misdoubt some evil;
Lest gaining gain on thee, and make thee dimme
To all things els. Wealth is the conjurers devil;
Whom when he thinks he hath, the devil hath him.
    Gold thou mayst safely touch; but if it stick
    Unto thy hands, it woundeth to the quick.

What skills it, if a bag of stones or gold
About thy neck do drown thee? raise thy head;
Take starres for money; starres not to be told
By any art, yet to be purchased.
    None is so wastefull as the scraping dame.
    She loseth three for one; her soul, rest, fame.

By no means runne in debt: take thine own measure.
Who cannot live on twentie pound a yeare,
Cannot on fourtie: he's a man of pleasure,
A kinde of thing that's for it self too deere.
    The curious unthrift makes his cloth too wide,
    And spares himself, but would his taylor chide.

*   *   *   *   *

Be calm in arguing: for fiercenesse makes
Errour a fault, and truth discourtesie.
Why should I feel another mans mistakes
More, then his sicknesses of povertie?
    In love I should: but anger is not love,
    Nor wisdome neither: therefore gently move.

Calmnesse is great advantage: he that lets
Another chafe, may warm him at his fire:
Mark all his wandrings, and enjoy his frets;
As cunning fencers suffer heat to tire.
    Truth dwels not in the clouds: the bow that's there,
    Doth often aim at, never hit the sphere.

*   *   *   *   *

None shall in hell such bitter pangs endure,
As those, who mock at Gods way of salvation.
Whom oil and balsames kill, what salve can cure?
They drink with greedinesse a full damnation.
 The Jews refused thunder; and we, folly.
 Though God do hedge us in, yet who is holy?

Summe up at night, what thou has done by day;
And in the morning, what thou hast to do.
Dresse and undresse thy soul: mark the decay
And growth of it: if with thy watch, that too
 Be down, then winde up both, since we shall be
 Most surely judg'd, make thy accounts agree.

In brief, acquit thee bravely; play the man.
Look not on pleasures as they come, but go.
Deferre not the least vertue: lifes poore span
Make not an ell, by trifling in thy wo.
 If thou do ill; the joy fades, not the pains:
 If well; the pain doth fade, the joy remains.

The Reprisall

 I have consider'd it, and finde
There is no dealing with thy mighty passion:
For though I die for thee, I am behinde;
 My sinnes deserve the condemnation.

 O make me innocent, that I
May give a disentangled state and free:
And yet thy wounds still my attempts defie,
 For by thy death I die for thee.

 Ah! was it not enough that thou
By thy eternall glorie didst outgo me?
Couldst thou not griefs sad conquests me allow,
 But in all vict'ries overthrow me?

Yet by confession will I come
Into the conquest. Though I can do nought
Against thee, in thee will I overcome
        The man who once against thee fought.

The Sinner

Lord, how I am all ague, when I seek
        What I have treasur'd in my memorie!
        Since, if my soul make even with the week,
Each seventh note by right is due to thee.
I finde there quarries of pil'd vanities,
        But shreds of holinesse, that dare not venture
        To shew their face, since crosse to thy decrees:
There the circumference earth is, heav'n the centre.
In so much dregs the quintessence is small:
        The spirit and good extract of my heart
        Comes to about the many hundredth part.
Yet Lord restore thine image, heare my call:
        And though my hard heart scarce to thee can grone,
        Remember that thou once didst write in stone.

Redemption

pure parable
tells story . shows us
beg. of 14th cent
v. feudal.

Having been tenant long to a rich Lord, a
    Not thriving, I resolved to be bold, b
    And make a suit unto him, to afford a
A new small-rented lease, and cancell th' old. b

In heaven at his manour I him sought: c
    They told me there, that he was lately gone d
    About some land, which he had dearly bought c
Long since on earth, to take possession. d

23

I straight return'd, and knowing his great birth,
    Sought him accordingly in great resorts;
    In cities, theatres, gardens, parks, and courts:
At length I heard a ragged noise and mirth

    Of theeves and murderers: there I him espied,
    Who straight, *Your suit is granted*, said, and died.

Easter

Rise heart; thy Lord is risen. Sing his praise
                Without delayes,
Who takes thee by the hand, that thou likewise
                With him mayst rise:
That, as his death calcined thee to dust,
His life may make thee gold, and much more just.

Awake, my lute, and struggle for thy part
                With all thy art.
The crosse taught all wood to resound his name,
                Who bore the same.
His streched sinews taught all strings, what key
Is best to celebrate this most high day.

Consort both heart and lute, and twist a song
                Pleasant and long:
Or since all musick is but three parts vied
                And multiplied;
O let thy blessed Spirit bear a part,
And make up our defects with his sweet art.

I got me flowers to straw thy way;
I got me boughs off many a tree:
But thou wast up by break of day,
And brought'st thy sweets along with thee.

24

The Sunne arising in the East,
Though he give light, & th' East perfume;
If they should offer to contest
With thy arising, they presume.

Can there be any day but this,
Though many sunnes to shine endeavour?
We count three hundred, but we misse:
There is but one, and that one ever.

Sinne

Lord, with what care hast thou begirt us round!
  Parents first season us: then schoolmasters
  Deliver us to laws; they send us bound
To rules of reason, holy messengers,

Pulpits and sundayes, sorrow dogging sinne,
  Afflictions sorted, anguish of all sizes,
  Fine nets and stratagems to catch us in,
Bibles laid open, millions of surprises,

Blessings beforehand, tyes of gratefulnesse,
  The sound of glorie ringing in our eares:
  Without, our shame; within, our consciences;
Angels and grace, eternall hopes and fears.

  Yet all these fences and their whole aray
  One cunning bosome-sinne blows quite away.

Repentance

Lord, I confesse my sinne is great;
Great is my sinne. Oh! gently treat
With thy quick flow'r, thy momentanie bloom;
    Whose life still pressing
    Is one undressing,
 A steadie aiming at a tombe.

Mans age is two houres work, or three:
Each day doth round about us see.
Thus are we to delights: but we are all
    To sorrows old,
    If life be told
From what life feeleth, Adams fall.

O let thy height of mercie then
Compassionate short-breathed men.
Cut me not off for my most foul transgression:
    I do confesse
    My foolishnesse;
My God, accept of my confession.

Sweeten at length this bitter bowl,
Which thou hast pour'd into my soul;
Thy wormwood turn to health, windes to fair weather:
    For if thou stay,
    I and this day,
As we did rise, we die together.

When thou for sinne rebukest man,
Forthwith he waxeth wo and wan:
Bitternesse fills our bowels; all our hearts
    Pine, and decay,
    And drop away,
And carrie with them th' other parts.

But thou wilt sinne and grief destroy;
That so the broken bones may joy,
And tune together in a well-set song,
Full of his praises,
Who dead men raises.
Fractures well cur'd make us more strong.

Prayer

Prayer the Churches banquet, Angels age,
Gods breath in man returning to his birth,
The soul in paraphrase, heart in pilgrimage,
The Christian plummet sounding heav'n and earth;

Engine against th' Almightie, sinners towre,
Reversed thunder, Christ-side-piercing spear,
The six-daies — world transposing in an houre,
A kinde of tune, which all things heare and fear;

Softnesse, and peace, and joy, and love, and blisse,
Exalted Manna, gladnesse of the best,
Heaven in ordinarie, man well drest,
The milkie may, the bird of Paradise,
Church-bels beyond the starres heard, the souls bloud,
The land of spices; something understood.

The H. Communion

Not in rich furniture, or fine aray,
Nor in a wedge of gold,
Thou, who from me wast sold,
To me dost now thy self convey;
For so thou should'st without me still have been,
Leaving within me sinne:

But by the way of nourishment and strength
          Thou creep'st into my breast;
          Making thy way my rest,
        And thy small quantities my length;
Which spread their forces into every part,
          Meeting sinnes force and art.

Yet can these not get over to my soul,
          Leaping the wall that parts
          Our souls and fleshly hearts;
        But as th' outworks, they may controll
My rebel-flesh, and carrying thy name,
          Affright both sinne and shame.

Onely thy grace, which with these elements comes,
          Knoweth the ready way,
          And hath the privie key,
        Op'ning the souls most subtile rooms;
While those to spirits refin'd, at doore attend
          Dispatches from their friend.

          Give me my captive soul, or take
            My bodie also thither.
          Another lift like this will make
            Them both to be together.

          Before that sinne turn'd flesh to stone,
            And all our lump to leaven;
          A fervent sigh might well have blown
            Our innocent earth to heaven.

          For sure when Adam did not know
            To sinne, or sinne to smother;
          He might to heav'n from Paradise go,
            As from one room t'another.

Thou hast restor'd us to this ease
By this thy heav'nly bloud;
Which I can go to, when I please,
And leave the earth to their food.

Love

I

Immortall Love, authour of this great frame,
Sprung from that beautie which can never fade;
How hath man parcel'd out thy glorious name,
And thrown it on that dust which thou hast made,

While mortall love doth all the title gain!
Which siding with invention, they together
Bear all the sway, possessing heart and brain,
(Thy workmanship) and give thee share in neither.

Wit fancies beautie, beautie raiseth wit:
The world is theirs; they two play out the game,
Thou standing by: and though thy glorious name
Wrought out deliverance from th' infernall pit,

Who sings thy praise? onely a skarf or glove
Doth warm our hands, and make them write of love.

II

Immortall Heat, O let thy greater flame
Attract the lesser to it: let those fires,
Which shall consume the world, first make it tame;
And kindle in our hearts such true desires,

As may consume our lusts, and make thee way.
Then shall our hearts pant thee; then shall our brain
All her invention on thine Altar lay,
And there in hymnes send back thy fire again:

29

Our eies shall see thee, which before saw dust;
    Dust blown by wit, till that they both were blinde:
    Thou shalt recover all thy goods in kinde,
Who wert disseized by usurping lust:

    All knees shall bow to thee; all wits shall rise,
    And praise him who did make and mend our eies.

Whitsunday

Listen sweet Dove unto my song,
And spread thy golden wings in me;
Hatching my tender heart so long,
Till it get wing, and flie away with thee.

Where is that fire which once descended
On thy Apostles? thou didst then
Keep open house, richly attended,
Feasting all comers by twelve chosen men.

Such glorious gifts thou didst bestow,
That th' earth did like a heav'n appeare;
The starres were coming down to know
If they might mend their wages, and serve here.

The sunne, which once did shine alone,
Hung down his head, and wisht for night,
When he beheld twelve sunnes for one
Going about the world, and giving light.

But since those pipes of gold, which brought
That cordiall water to our ground,
Were cut and martyr'd by the fault
Of those, who did themselves through their side wound.

Thou shutt'st the doore, and keep'st within;
Scarce a good joy creeps through the chink:
And if the braves of conqu'ring sinne
Did not excite thee, we should wholly sink.

Lord, though we change, thou art the same;
The same sweet God of love and light:
Restore this day, for thy great name,
Unto his ancient and miraculous right.

Grace

My stock lies dead, and no increase
Doth my dull husbandrie improve:
O let thy graces without cease
      Drop from above!

If still the sunne should hide his face,
Thy house would but a dangeon prove,
Thy works nights captives: O let grace
      Drop from above!

The dew doth ev'ry morning fall;
And shall the dew out-strip thy dove?
The dew, for which grasse cannot call,
      Drop from above.

Death is still working like a mole,
And digs my grave at each remove:
Let grace work too, and on my soul
      Drop from above.

Sinne is still hammering my heart
Unto a hardnesse, void of love:
Let suppling grace, to crosse his art,
      Drop from above.

O come ! for thou dost know the way.
Or if to me thou wilt not move,
Remove me, where I need not say,
          Drop from above.

Mattens

I cannot ope mine eyes,
But thou art ready there to catch
My morning-soul and sacrifice :
Then we must needs for that day make a match.

          My God, what is a heart?
          Silver, or gold, or precious stone,
          Or starre, or rainbow, or a part
Of all these things, or all of them in one?

          My God, what is a heart,
          That thou should'st it so eye, and wooe,
          Powring upon it all thy art,
As if that thou hadst nothing els to do?

          Indeed mans whole estate
          Amounts (and richly) to serve thee :
          He did not heav'n and earth create,
Yet studies them, not him by whom they be.

          Teach me thy love to know ;
          That this new light, which now I see,
          May both the work and workman show :
Then by a sunne-beam I will climbe to thee.

32

The Windows

Lord, how can man preach thy eternall word?
        He is a brittle crazie glasse:
Yet in thy temple thou dost him afford
        This glorious and transcendent place,
        To be a window, through thy grace.

But when thou dost anneal in glasse thy storie,
        Making thy life to shine within
The holy Preachers; then the light and glorie
        More rev'rend grows, and more doth win:
        Which else shows watrish, bleak, and thin.

Doctrine and life, colours and light, in one
        When they combine and mingle, bring
A strong regard and aw: but speech alone
        Doth vanish like a flaring thing,
        And in the eare, not conscience ring.

Content

Peace mutt'ring thoughts, and do not grudge to keep
        Within the walls of your own breast:
Who cannot on his own bed sweetly sleep,
        Can on anothers hardly rest.

Gad not abroad at ev'ry quest and call
        Of an untrained hope or passion.
To court each place or fortune that doth fall,
        Is wantonnesse in contemplation.

Mark how the fire in flints doth quiet lie,
        Content and warm t' it self alone:
But when it would appeare to others eye,
        Without a knock it never shone.

Give me the pliant minde, whose gentle measure
      Complies and suits with all estates;
Which can let loose to a crown, and yet with pleasure
      Take up within a cloisters gates.

This soul doth span the world, and hang content
      From either pole unto the centre:
Where in each room of the well-furnisht tent
      He lies warm, and without adventure.

The brags of life are but a nine dayes wonder;
      And after death the fumes that spring
From private bodies, make as big a thunder,
      As those which rise from a huge King.

Onely thy Chronicle is lost; and yet
      Better by worms be all once spent,
Then to have hellish moths still gnaw and fret
      Thy name in books, which may not rent:

When all thy deeds, whose brunt thou feel'st alone,
      Are chaw'd by others pens and tongues;
And as their wit is, their digestion,
      Thy nourisht fame is weak or strong.

Then cease discoursing soul, till thine own ground,
      Do not thy self or friends importune.
He that by seeking hath himself once found,
      Hath euer found a happie fortune.

Constancie

    Who is the honest man?
He that doth still and strongly good pursue,
To God, his neighbour, and himself most true:
    Whom neither force nor fawning can
Unpinne, or wrench from giving all their due.

Whose honestie is not
So loose or easie, that a ruffling winde
Can blow away, or glittering look it blinde:
    Who rides his sure and even trot,
While the world now rides by, now lags behinde.

    Who, when great trials come,
Nor seeks, nor shunnes them; but doth calmly stay,
Till he the thing and the example weigh:
    All being brought into a summe,
What place or person calls for, he doth pay.

    Whom none can work or wooe
To use in any thing a trick or sleight,
For above all things he abhorres deceit:
    His words and works and fashion too
All of a piece, and all are cleare and straight.

    Who never melts or thaws
At close tentations: when the day is done,
His goodnesse sets not, but in dark can runne:
    The sunne to others writeth laws,
And is their vertue; Vertue is his Sunne.

    Who, when he is to treat
With sick folks, women, those whom passions sway,
Allows for that, and keeps his constant way:
    Whom others faults do not defeat;
But though men fail him, yet his part doth play.

    Whom nothing can procure,
When the wide world runnes bias, from his will
To writhe his limbes, and share, not mend the ill.
    This is the Mark-man, safe and sure,
Who still is right, and prayes to be so still.

The Starre *v. original*

Bright spark, shot from a brighter place,　　*4*
　Where beams surround my Saviours face,　*4*
　　Canst thou be any where　　*3*
　　　So well as there?　　*2*

Yet, if thou wilt from thence depart,
　Take a bad lodging in my heart;
　　For thou canst make a debter,
　　　And make it better.

First with thy fire-work burn to dust
　Folly, and worse then folly, lust:
　　Then with thy light refine,
　　　And make it shine:

So disengag'd from sinne and sicknesse,
　Touch it with thy celestiall quicknesse,
　　That it may hang and move
　　　After thy love.

Then with our trinitie of light,
　Motion, and heat, let's take our flight
　　Unto the place where thou
　　　Before didst bow.

Get me a standing there, and place
　Among the beams, which crown the face
　　Of him, who dy'd to part
　　　Sinne and my heart:

That so among the rest I may
　Glitter, and curle, and winde as they:
　　That winding is their fashion
　　　Of adoration.

Sure thou wilt joy, by gaining me
To flie home like a laden bee
Unto that hive of beams
And garland-streams.

Sunday

O day most calm, most bright,
The fruit of this, the next worlds bud,
Th' indorsement of supreme delight,
Writ by a friend, and with his bloud;
The couch of time; cares balm and bay:
The week were dark, but for thy light:
       Thy torch doth show the way.

The other dayes and thou
Make up one man; whose face thou art,
Knocking at heaven with thy brow:
The worky-daies are the back-part;
The burden of the week lies there,
Making the whole to stoup and bow,
       Till thy release appeare.

       Man had straight forward gone
To endlesse death: but thou dost pull
And turn us round to look on one,
Whom, if we were not very dull,
We could not choose but look on still;
Since there is no place so alone,
       The which he doth not fill.

       Sundaies the pillars are,
On which heav'ns palace arched lies:
The other dayes fill up the spare
And hollow room with vanities.

They are the fruitful beds and borders
In Gods rich garden: that is bare,
      Which parts their ranks and orders.

      The Sundaies of mans life,
Thredded together on times string,
Make bracelets to adorn the wife
Of the eternall glorious King.
On Sunday heavens gate stands ope;
Blessings are plentifull and rife,
      More plentifull then hope.

      This day my Saviour rose,
And did inclose this light for his:
That, as each beast his manger knows,
Man might not of his fodder misse.
Christ hath took in this piece of ground,
And made a garden there for those
      Who want herbs for their wound.

      The rest of our Creation
Our great Redeemer did remove
With the same shake, which at his passion
Did th' earth and all things with it move.
As Samson bore the doores away,
Christs hands, though nail'd, wrought our salvation,
      And did unhinge that day.

      The brightnesse of that day
We sullied by our foul offence:
Wherefore that robe we cast away,
Having a new at his expence,
Whose drops of bloud paid the full price,
That was requir'd to make us gay,
      And fit for Paradise.

Thou art a day of mirth:
And where the week-dayes trail on ground,
Thy flight is higher, as thy birth.
O let me take thee at the bound,
Leaping with thee from sev'n to sev'n,
Till that we both, being toss'd from earth,
    Flie hand in hand to heav'n!

Employment

He that is weary, let him sit.
    My soul would stirre
And trade in courtesies and wit,
    Quitting the furre
To cold complexions needing it.

Man is no starre, but a quick coal
    Of mortall fire:
Who blows it not, nor doth controll
    A faint desire,
Lets his own ashes choke his soul.

When th' elements did for place contest
    With him, whose will
Ordain'd the highest to be best;
    The earth sat still,
And by the others is opprest.

Life is a businesse, not good cheer;
    Ever in warres.
The sunne still shineth there or here,
    Whereas the starres
Watch an advantage to appeare.

39

Oh that I were an Orenge-tree,
        That busie plant !
Then should I ever laden be,
        And never want
Some fruit for him that dressed me.

But we are still too young or old;
        The man is gone,
Before we do our wares unfold:
        So we freeze on,
Until the grave increase our cold.

Christmas

All after pleasures as I rid one day,
    My horse and I, both tir'd, bodie and minde,
    With full crie of affections, quite astray;
I took up in the next inne I could finde.

There when I came, whom found I but my deare,
    My dearest Lord, expecting till the grief
    Of pleasures brought me to him, readie there
To be all passengers most sweet relief?

O Thou, whose glorious, yet contracted light,
    Wrapt in nights mantle, stole into a manger;
    Since my dark soul and brutish is thy right,
To Man of all beasts be not thou a stranger:
    Furnish and deck my soul, that thou mayst have
    A better lodging, then a rack, or grave.

The shepherds sing; and shall I silent be?
        My God, no hymne for thee?
My soul's a shepherd too; a flock it feeds
        Of thoughts, and words, and deeds.

The pasture is thy word : the streams, thy grace
        Enriching all the place.
Shepherd and flock shall sing, and all my powers
        Out-sing the day-light houres.
Then we will chide the sunne for letting night
        Take up his place and right :
We sing one common Lord ; wherefore he should
        Himself the candle hold.
I will go searching, till I finde a sunne
        Shall stay, till we have done ;
A willing shiner, that shall shine as gladly,
        As frost-nipt sunnes look sadly.
Then we will sing, and shine all our own day,
        And one another pay :
His beams shall cheer my breast, and both so twine,
Till ev'n his beams sing, and my musick shine.

Sighs and Grones

        O do not use me
After my sinnes ! look not on my desert,
But on thy glorie ! then thou wilt reform
And not refuse me : for thou onely art
The mightie God, but I a sillie worm ;
        O do not bruise me !

        O do not urge me !
For what account can thy ill steward make ?
I have abus'd thy stock, destroy'd thy woods,
Suckt all thy magazens : my head did ake,
Till it found out how to consume thy goods :
        O do not scourge me !

O do not blinde me!
I have deserv'd that an Egyptian night
Should thicken all my powers; because my lust
Hath still sow'd fig-leaves to exclude thy light:
But I am frailtie, and already dust;
O do not grinde me!

O do not fill me
With the turn'd viall of thy bitter wrath!
For thou hast other vessels full of bloud,
A part whereof my Saviour empti'd hath,
Ev'n unto death: since he di'd for my good,
O do not kill me!

But O reprieve me!
For thou hast *life* and *death* at thy command;
Thou art both *Judge* and *Saviour, feast* and *rod,*
Cordiall and *Corrosive*: put not thy hand
Into the bitter box; but O my God,
My God, relieve me!

Vertue

Sweet day, so cool, so calm, so bright,
The bridall of the earth and skie:
The dew shall weep thy fall to night;
For thou must die.

Sweet rose, whose hue angrie and brave
Bids the rash gazer wipe his eye:
Thy root is ever in its grave,
And thou must die.

Sweet spring, full of sweet dayes and roses,
A box where sweets compacted lie;
My musick shows ye have your closes,
And all must die.

42

Onely a sweet and vertuous soul,
Like season'd timber, never gives;
But though the whole world turn to coal, *He wants it*
        Then chiefly lives. *to jar.*

Wants to bring in idea of continuity.

individual ## Man

      My God, I heard this day, *a*
That none doth build a stately habitation, *b*
      But he that means to dwell therein. *c*
      What house more stately hath there been,
Or can be, then is Man? to whose creation *b*
        All things are in decay. *a*

       For Man is ev'ry thing,
And more: He is a tree, yet bears no fruit;
      A beast, yet is, or should be more:
      Reason and speech we onely bring.
Parrats may thank us, if they are not mute,
        They go upon the score.

       Man is all symmetrie,
Full of proportions, one limbe to another,
      And all to all the world besides:
      Each part may call the farthest, brother:
For head with foot hath private amitie,
        And both with moons and tides.

       Nothing hath got so farre,
But Man hath caught and kept it, as his prey.
      His eyes dismount the highest starre:
      He is in little all the sphere.
Herbs gladly cure our flesh; because that they
        Finde their acquaintance there.

43

however poetical Herbert is he is so always conversational

haven't been uplifted by Totalitarian

rhyme scheme

physical symmetry

For us the windes do blow,
The earth doth rest, heav'n move, and fountains flow.
    Nothing we see, but means our good,
      As our *delight*, or as our *treasure*:
The whole is, either our cupboard of *food*,
      Or cabinet of *pleasure*.

    The starres have us to bed;
Night draws the curtain, which the sunne withdraws;
    Musick and light attend our head.
    All things unto our *flesh* are kinde
In their *descent* and *being*; to our *minde*
    In their *ascent* and *cause*.

    Each thing is full of dutie:
Waters united are our navigation;
    Distinguished, our habitation;
    Below, our drink; above, our meat;
Both are our cleanlinesse. Hath one such beautie?
    Then how are all things neat?

    More servants wait on Man,
Then he'l take notice of: in ev'ry path
    He treads down that which doth befriend him,
    When sicknesse makes him pale and wan.
Oh mightie love! Man is one world, and hath
    Another to attend him.

    Since then, my God, thou hast
So brave a Palace built; O dwell in it,
    That it may dwell with thee at last!
    Till then, afford us so much wit;
That, as the world serves us, we may serve thee,
    And both thy servants be.

Unkindnesse

Lord, make me coy and tender to offend :
In friendship, first I think, if that agree,
         Which I intend,
    Unto my friends intent and end.
I would not use a friend, as I use Thee.

If any touch my friend, or his good name ;
It is my honour and my love to free
         His blasted fame
    From the least spot or thought of blame.
I could not use a friend, as I use Thee.

My friend may spit upon my curious floore:
Would he have gold? I lend it instantly ;
         But let the poore,
    And thou within them starve at doore.
I cannot use a friend, as I use Thee.

When that my friend pretendeth to a place,
I quit my interest, and leave it free :
         But when thy grace
    Sues for my heart, I thee displace,
Nor would I use a friend, as I use Thee.

Yet can a friend what thou hast done fulfill?
O write in brasse, *My God upon a tree*
         His bloud did spill
    Onely to purchase my good-will :
Yet use I not my foes, as I use thee.

Life

I made a posie, while the day ran by:
Here will I smell my remnant out, and tie
        My life within this band.
But time did becken to the flowers, and they
By noon most cunningly did steal away,
        And wither'd in my hand.

My hand was next to them, and then my heart:
I took, without more thinking, in good part
        Times gentle admonition:
Who did so sweetly deaths sad taste convey,
Making my minde to smell my fatall day;
        Yet sugring the suspicion.

Farewell deare flowers, sweetly your time ye spent,
Fit, while ye liv'd, for smell or ornament,
        And after death for cures
I follow straight without complaints or grief,
Since if my sent be good, I care not, if
        It be as short as yours.

Home

Come, Lord, my head doth burn, my heart is sick,
        While thou dost ever, ever stay:
Thy long deferrings wound me to the quick,
        My spirit gaspeth night and day.
        O show thy self to me,
        Or take me up to thee!

How canst thou stay, considering the pace
        The bloud did make, which thou didst waste?
When I behold it trickling down thy face,
        I never saw thing make such haste.
        O show thy, &c.

When man was lost, thy pitie lookt about
　　　　To see what help in th' earth or skie:
But there was none; at least no help without:
　　　　The help did in thy bosome lie.
　　　　　　O show thy self to me,
　　　　　　Or take me up to thee!

There lay thy sonne: and must he leave that nest,
　　　　That hive of sweetnesse, to remove
Thraldome from those, who would not at a feast
　　　　Leave one poore apple for thy love?
　　　　　　O show thy, &c.

He did, he came: O my Redeemer deare,
　　　　After all this canst thou be strange?
So many yeares baptiz'd, and not appeare?
　　　　As if thy love could fail or change.
　　　　　　O show thy, &c.

Yet if thou stayest still, why must I stay?
　　　　My God, what is this world to me?
This world of wo? hence all ye clouds, away,
　　　　Away; I must get up and see.
　　　　　　O show thy, &c.

What is this weary world; this meat and drink,
　　　　That chains us by the teeth so fast?
What is this woman-kinde, which I can wink
　　　　Into a blacknesse and distaste?
　　　　　　O show thy, &c.

With one small sigh thou gav'st me th' other day
　　　　I blasted all the joyes about me:
And scouling on them as they pin'd away,
　　　　Now come again, said I, and flout me.
　　　　　　O show thy, &c.

Nothing but drought and dearth, but bush and brake,
　　Which way so-e're I look, I see.
Some may dream merrily, but when they wake,
　　They dresse themselves and come to thee.
　　　　O show thy self to me,
　　　　Or take me up to thee!

We talk of harvests; there are no such things,
　　But when we leave our corn and hay:
There is no fruitful yeare, but that which brings
　　The last and lov'd, though dreadfull day.
　　　　O show thy, &c.

Oh loose this frame, this knot of man untie!
　　That my free soul may use her wing,
Which now is pinion'd with mortalitie,
　　As an intangled, hamper'd thing.
　　　　O show thy, &c.

What have I left, that I should stay and grone?
　　The most of me to heav'n is fled:
My thoughts and joyes are all packt up and gone,
　　And for their old acquaintance plead.
　　　　O show thy, &c.

Come dearest Lord, pass not this holy season,
　　My flesh and bones and joynts do pray:
And ev'n my verse, when by the ryme and reason
　　The word is, *Stay*, sayes ever, *Come*.
　　　　O show thy, &c.

The Quip

The merrie world did on a day
With his train-bands and mates agree
To meet together, where I lay
And all in sport to geere at me.

48

First, Beautie crept into a rose,
Which when I pluckt not, Sir, said she,
Tell me, I pray, Whose hands are those?
But thou shalt answer, Lord, for me.

Then Money came, and chinking still,
What tune is this, poore man? said he:
I heard in Musick you had skill.
But thou shalt answer, Lord, for me.

Then came brave Glorie puffing by
In silks that whistled, who but he?
He scarce allow'd me half an eie.
But thou shalt answer, Lord, for me.

Then came quick Wit and Conversation,
And he would needs a comfort be,
And, to be short, make an oration.
But thou shalt answer, Lord, for me.

Yet when the houre of thy designe
To answer these fine things shall come;
Speak not at large, say, I am thine:
And then they have their answer home.

Dialogue

Sweetest Saviour, if my soul
    Were but worth the having,
Quickly should I then controll
    Any thought of waving.
But when all my care and pains
Cannot give the name of gains
To thy wretch so full of stains;
What delight or hope remains?

What (childe) is the ballance thine,
  Thine the poise and measure?
If I say, Thou shalt be mine;
  Finger not my treasure.
What the gains in having thee
Do amount to, onely he,
Who for man was sold, can see;
That transferr'd th' accounts to me.

But as I can see no merit,
  Leading to this favour:
So the way to fit me for it,
  Is beyond my savour.
As the reason then is thine;
So the way is none of mine:
I disclaim the whole designe:
Sinne disclaims and I resigne.

That is all, if that I could
  Get without repining;
And my clay my creature would
  Follow my resigning.
That as I did freely part
With my glorie and desert,
Left all joyes to feel all smart—
  Ah! no more: thou break'st my heart.

Providence

O Sacred Providence, who from end to end
Strongly and sweetly movest! shall I write,
And not of thee, through whom my fingers bend
To hold my quill? shall they not do thee right?

Of all the creatures both in sea and land
Onely to Man thou hast made known thy wayes,
And put the penne alone into his hand,
And made him Secretarie of thy praise.

Beasts fain would sing; birds dittie to their notes;
Trees would be tuning on their native lute
To thy renown: but all their hands and throats
Are brought to Man, while they are lame and mute.

Man is the worlds high Priest: he doth present
The sacrifice for all; while they below
Unto the service mutter an assent,
Such as springs use that fall, and windes that blow.

He that to praise and laud thee doth refrain,
Doth not refrain unto himself alone,
But robs a thousand who would praise thee fain,
And doth commit a world of sinne in one.

The beasts say, Eat me: but, if beasts must teach,
The tongue is yours to eat, but mine to praise.
The trees say, Pull me: but the hand you stretch,
Is mine to write, as it is yours to raise.

Wherefore, most sacred Spirit, I here present
For me and all my fellows praise to thee:
And just it is that I should pay the rent,
Because the benefit accrues to me.

We all acknowledge both thy power and love
To be exact, transcendent, and divine;
Who dost so strongly and so sweetly move,
While all things have their will, yet none but thine.

For either thy *command*, or thy *permission*
Lay hands on all: they are thy *right* and *left*.
The first puts on with speed and expedition;
The other curbs sinnes stealing pace and theft.

Nothing escapes them both; all must appeare,
And be dispos'd, and dress'd, and tun'd by thee,
Who sweetly temper'st all. If we could heare
Thy skill and art, what musick would it be!

Thou art in small things great, not small in any:
Thy even praise can neither rise, nor fall.
Thou art in all things one, in each thing many:
For thou art infinite in one and all.

Tempests are calm to thee; they know thy hand,
And hold it fast, as children do their fathers,
Which crie and follow. Thou hast made poore sand
Check the proud sea, ev'n when it swells and gathers.

Thy cupboard serves the world: the meat is set,
Where all may reach: no beast but knows his feed.
Birds teach us hawking; fishes have their net:
The great prey on the lesse, they on some weed.

Nothing ingendred doth prevent his meat:
Flies have their table spread, ere they appeare.
Some creatures have in winter what to eat;
Others do sleep, and envie not their cheer.

How finely dost thou times and seasons spin,
And make a twist checker'd with night and day!
Which as it lengthens windes, and windes us in,
As bouls go on, but turning all the way.

Each creature hath a wisdome for his good.
The pigeons feed their tender off-spring, crying,
When they are callow; but withdraw their food
When they are fledge, that need may teach the flying.

Bees work for man; and yet they never bruise
Their masters flowers, but leave it, having done,
As fair as ever, and as fit to use;
So both the flower doth stay, and hony run.

Sheep eat the grasse, and dung the ground for more:
Trees after bearing drop their leaves for soil:
Springs vent their streams, and by expense get store:
Clouds cool by heat, and baths by cooling boil.

Who hath the vertue to expresse the rare
And curious vertues both of herbs and stones?
Is there an herb for that? O that thy care
Would show a root, that gives expressions!

And if an herb hath power, what have the starres?
A rose, besides his beautie, is a cure.
Doubtlesse our plagues and plentie, peace and warres
Are there much surer then our art is sure.

Thou hast hid metals: man may take them thence;
But at his peril: when he digs the place,
He makes a grave; as if the thing had sense,
And threatned man, that he should fill the space.

Ev'n poysons praise thee. Should a thing be lost?
Should creatures want for want of heed their due?
Since where are poysons, antidots are most:
The help stands close, and keeps the fear in view.

The sea, which seems to stop the traveller,
Is by a ship the speedier passage made.
The windes, who think they rule the mariner,
Are rul'd by him, and taught to serve his trade.

And as thy house is full, so I adore
Thy curious art in marshalling thy goods.
The hills with health abound; the vales with store;
The South with marble; North with furres & woods.

Hard things are glorious; easie things good cheap.
The common all men have; that which is rare,
Men therefore seek to have, and care to keep.
The healthy frosts with summer-fruits compare.

Light without winde is glasse: warm without weight
Is wooll and furres: cool without closenesse, shade:
Speed without pains, a horse: tall without height,
A servile hawk: low without losse, a spade.

All countreys have enough to serve their need:
If they seek fine things, thou dost make them run
For their offence; and then dost turn their speed
To be commerce and trade from sunne to sunne.

Nothing wears clothes, but Man; nothing doth need
But he to wear them. Nothing useth fire,
But Man alone, to show his heav'nly breed:
And onely he hath fuell in desire.

When th' earth was dry, thou mad'st a sea of wet:
Whẽ that lay gather'd, thou didst broach the moũtains:
When yet some places could no moisture get,
The windes grew gard'ners, and the clouds good fountains.

Rain, do not hurt my flowers; but gently spend
Your hony drops: presse not to smell them here:
When they are ripe, their odour will ascend,
And at your lodging with their thanks appeare.

How harsh are thorns to pears! and yet they make
A better hedge, and need lesse reparation.
How smooth are silks compared with a stake,
Or with a stone! yet make no good foundation.

Sometimes thou dost divide thy gifts to man,
Sometimes unite. The Indian nut alone
Is clothing, meat and trencher, drink and kan,
Boat, cable, sail and needle, all in one.

Most herbs that grow in brooks, are hot and dry.
Cold fruits warm kernells help against the winde.
The lemmons juice and rinde cure mutually.
The whey of milk doth loose, the milk doth binde.

Thy creatures leap not, but expresse a feast,
Where all the guests sit close, and nothing wants.
Frogs marry fish and flesh; bats, bird and beast;
Sponges, non-sense and sense; mines, th' earth & plants.

To show thou art not bound, as if thy lot
Were worse then ours; sometimes thou shiftest hands.
Most things move th' under-jaw; the Crocodile not.
Most things sleep lying; th' Elephant leans or stands.

But who hath praise enough? nay who hath any?
None can expresse thy works, but he that knows them:
And none can know thy works, which are so many,
And so complete, but onely he that owes them.

All things that are, though they have sev'rall wayes,
Yet in their being joyn with one advise
To honour thee: and so I give thee praise
In all my other hymnes, but in this twice.

Each thing that is, although in use and name
It go for one, hath many wayes in store
To honour thee; and so each hymne thy fame
Extolleth many wayes, yet this one more.

Hope

I gave to Hope a watch of mine: but he
             An anchor gave to me.
Then an old prayer-book I did present:
             And he an optick sent.
With that I gave a viall full of tears:
             But he a few green eares:
Ah Loyterer! I'le no more, no more I'le bring:
             I did expect a ring.

Sinnes·Round

Sorrie I am, my God, sorrie I am,
That my offences course it in a ring.
My thoughts are working like a busie flame,
Untill their cockatrice they hatch and bring:
And when they once have perfected their draughts,
My words take fire from my inflamed thoughts.

My words take fire from my inflamed thoughts,
Which spit it forth like the Sicilian hill.
They vent the wares, and passe them with their faults,
And by their breathing ventilate the ill.
But words suffice not, where are lewd intentions:
My hands do joyn to finish the inventions.

My hands do joyn to finish the inventions:
And so my sinnes ascend three stories high,
As Babel grew, before there were dissentions.
Yet ill deeds loyter not: for they supplie
New thoughts of sinning: wherefore, to my shame,
Sorrie I am, my God, sorrie I am.

Time

Meeting with Time, slack thing, said I,
Thy sithe is dull; whet it for shame.
No marvell Sir, he did replie,
If it at length deserve some blame:
    But where one man would have me grinde it,
    Twentie for one too sharp do finde it.

Perhaps some such of old did passe,
Who above all things lov'd this life;
To whom thy sithe a hatchet was,
Which now is but a pruning-knife.
  Christs coming hath made man thy debter,
  Since by thy cutting he grows better.

And in his blessing thou art blest:
For where thou onely wert before
An executioner at best;
Thou art a gard'ner now, and more,
  An usher to convey our souls
  Beyond the utmost starres and poles.

And this is that makes life so long,
While it detains us from our God.
Ev'n pleasures here increase the wrong,
And length of dayes lengthen the rod.
  Who wants the place, where God doth dwell,
  Partakes already half of hell.

Of what strange length must that needs be,
Which ev'n eternitie excludes!
Thus farre Time heard me patiently:
Then chafing said, This man deludes:
  What do I here before his doore?
  He doth not crave lesse time, but more.

Gratefulnesse

Thou that hast giv'n so much to me,
Give one thing more, a gratefull heart.
See how thy beggar works on thee
                    By art.

He makes thy gifts occasion more,
And sayes, If he in this be crost,
All thou hast giv'n him heretofore
                              Is lost.

But thou didst reckon, when at first
Thy word our hearts and hands did crave,
What it would come to at the worst
                              To save.

Perpetuall knockings at thy doore,
Tears sullying thy transparent rooms,
Gift upon gift, much would have more,
                              And comes.

This not withstanding, thou wentst on,
And didst allow us all our noise:
Nay thou hast made a sigh and grone
                              Thy joyes.

Not that thou hast not still above
Much better tunes, then grones can make;
But that these countrey-aires thy love
                              Did take.

Wherefore I crie, and crie again;
And in no quiet canst thou be,
Till I a thankfull heart obtain
                              Of thee:

Not thankfull, when it pleaseth me;
As if thy blessings had spare dayes:
But such a heart, whose pulse may be
                              Thy praise.

Peace

Sweet Peace, where dost thou dwell? I humbly crave,
              Let me once know.
       I sought thee in a secret cave,
              And ask'd, if Peace were there.
A hollow winde did seem to answer, No:
              Go seek elsewhere.

I did; and going did a rainbow note:
              Surely, thought I,
       This is the lace of Peaces coat:
              I will search out the matter.
But while I lookt, the clouds immediately
              Did break and scatter.

Then went I to a garden, and did spy
              A gallant flower,
       The crown Imperiall: Sure, said I,
              Peace at the root must dwell.
But when I digg'd, I saw a worm devoure
              What show'd so well.

At length I met a rev'rend good old man,
              Whom when for Peace
       I did demand; he thus began:
              There was a Prince of old
At Salem dwelt, who liv'd with good increase
              Of flock and fold.

He sweetly liv'd; yet sweetnesse did not save
              His life from foes.
       But after death out of his grave
              There sprang twelve stalks of wheat:
Which many wondring at, got some of those
              To plant and set.

It prosper'd strangely, and did soon disperse
                    Through all the earth:
            For they that taste it do rehearse,
                That vertue lies therein,
A secret vertue bringing peace and mirth
                    By flight of sinne.

Take of this grain, which in my garden grows,
                    And grows for you;
            Make bread of it: and that repose
                And peace which ev'ry where
With so much earnestnesse you do pursue,
                    Is onely there.

Mans Medley

Heark, how the birds do sing,
                And woods do ring.
All creatures have their joy: and man hath his.
            Yet if we rightly measure,
                Mans joy and pleasure
Rather hereafter, then in present, is.

            To this life things of sense
                Make their pretence:
In th'other Angels have a right by birth:
            Man ties them both alone,
                And makes them one,
With th'one hand touching heav'n, with th'other earth.

            In soul he mounts and flies,
                In flesh he dies.
He wears a stuffe whose thread is course and round,
            But trimm'd with curious lace,
                And should take place
After the trimming, not the stuffe and ground.

Not, that he may not here
Taste of the cheer,
But as birds drink, and straight lift up their head,
So must he sip and think
Of better drink
He may attain to, after he is dead.

But as his joyes are double;
So is his trouble.
He hath two winters, other things but one:
Both frosts and thoughts do nip,
And bite his lip;
And he of all things fears two deaths alone.

Yet ev'n the greatest griefs
May be reliefs,
Could he but take them right, and in their wayes.
Happie is he, whose heart
Hath found the art
To turn his double pains to double praise.

The Method

Poore heart, lament.
For since thy God refuseth still,
There is some rub, some discontent,
Which cools his will.

Thy Father *could*
Quickly effect, what thou dost move;
For he is *Power*: and sure he *would*;
For he is *Love*.

Go search this thing,
Tumble thy breast, and turn thy book.
If thou hadst lost a glove or ring,
Wouldst thou not look?

61

What do I see
Written above there! *Yesterday*
I did behave me carelessly,
When I did pray.

And should Gods eare
To such indifferents chained be,
Who do not their own motions heare?
Is God lesse free?

But stay! what's there?
Late when I would have something done,
I had a motion to forbear,
Yet I went on.

And should God's eare,
Which needs not man, be ty'd to those
Who heare not him, but quickly heare
His utter foes?

Then once more pray:
Down with thy knees, up with thy voice.
Seek pardon first, and God will say,
Glad heart rejoyce.

The Pilgrimage

I travell'd on, seeing the hill, where lay
My expectation.
A long it was and weary way
The gloomy cave of Desperation
I left on th' one, and on the other side
The rock of Pride.

And so I came to phansies medow strow'd
                         With many a flower:
         Fain would I here have made abode,
         But I was quicken'd by my houre.
So to cares cops I came, and there got through
                         With much ado.

That led me to the wilde of passion, which
                         Some call the wold;
         A wasted place, but sometimes rich.
         Here I was robb'd of all my gold,
Save one good Angell, which a friend had ti'd
                         Close to my side.

At length I got unto the gladsome hill,
                         Where lay my hope,
         Where lay my heart; and climbing still,
         When I had gain'd the brow and top,
A lake of brackish waters on the ground
                         Was all I found.

With that abash'd and struck with many a sting
                         Of swarming fears,
         I fell, and cry'd, Alas my King;
         Can both the way and end be tears?
Yet taking heart I rose, and then perceiv'd
                         I was deceiv'd:

My hill was further: so I flung away,
                         Yet heard a crie
         Just as I went, *None goes that way*
         And lives: If that be all, said I,
After so foul a journey death is fair,
                         And but a chair.

Praise

King of Glorie, King of Peace,
　　　I will love thee:
And that love may never cease,
　　　I will move thee.

Thou hast granted my request,
　　　Thou hast heard me:
Thou didst note my working breast,
　　　Thou hast spar'd me.

Wherefore with my utmost art
　　　I will sing thee,
And the cream of all my heart
　　　I will bring thee.

Though my sinnes against me cried,
　　　Thou didst cleare me;
And alone, when they replied,
　　　Thou didst heare me.

Sev'n whole dayes, not one in seven,
　　　I will praise thee.
In my heart, though not in heaven,
　　　I can raise thee.

Thou grew'st soft and moist with tears,
　　　Thou relentedst:
And when Justice call'd for fears,
　　　Thou dissentedst.

Small it is, in this poore sort
　　　To enroll thee:
Ev'n eternitie is too short
　　　To extoll thee.

The Bag

Away despair; my gracious Lord doth heare.
  Though windes and waves assault my keel,
  He doth preserve it: he doth steer,
  Ev'n when the boat seems most to reel.
  Storms are the triumph of his art:
Well may he close his eyes, but not his heart.

Hast thou not heard, that my Lord Jesus di'd?
  Then let me tell thee a strange storie.
  The God of power, as he did ride
  In his majestick robes of glorie,
  Resolv'd to light; and so one day
He did descend, undressing all the way.

The starres his tire of light and rings obtain'd,
  The cloud his bow, the fire his spear,
  The sky his azure mantle gain'd.
  And when they ask'd, what he would wear;
  He smil'd and said as he did go,
He had new clothes a making here below.

When he was come, as travellers are wont,
  He did repair unto an inne.
  Both then, and after, many a brunt
  He did endure to cancell sinne:
  And having giv'n the rest before,
Here he gave up his life to pay our score.

But as he was returning, there came one
  That ran upon him with a spear.
  He, who came hither all alone,
  Bringing nor man, nor arms, nor fear,
  Receiv'd the blow upon his side,
And straight he turn'd, and to his brethren cry'd,

If ye have any thing to send or write,
    (I have no bag, but here is room)
    Unto my fathers hands and sight
    (Beleeve me) it shall safely come,
    That I shall minde, what you impart;
Look, you may put it very neare my heart.

Or if hereafter any of my friends
    Will use me in this kinde, the doore
    Shall still be open; what he sends
    I will present, and somewhat more,
    Not to his hurt. Sighs will convey
Any thing to me. Heark despair, away.

The Collar

I struck the board, and cry'd, No more.
    I will abroad.
What? shall I ever sigh and pine?
My lines and life are free; free as the rode,
    Loose as the winde, as large as store.
      Shall I be still in suit?
Have I no harvest but a thorn
    To let me bloud, and not restore
What I have lost with cordiall fruit?
      Sure there was wine
Before my sighs did drie it: there was corn
    Before my tears did drown it.
Is the yeare onely lost to me?
    Have I no bayes to crown it?
No flowers, no garlands gay? all blasted?
      All wasted?
Not so, my heart: but there is fruit,
      And thou hast hands.
Recover all thy sigh-blown age
On double pleasures: leave thy cold dispute

66

mastery of rhythm.

Of what is fit, and not. Forsake thy cage,
                Thy rope of sands,
Which pettie thoughts have made, and made to thee
    Good cable, to enforce and draw,
                And be thy law,
  While thou didst wink and wouldst not see.
                Away; take heed:
                I will abroad.
Call in thy deaths head there: tie up thy fears.
                He that forbears
      To suit and serve his need,
              Deserves his load.
But as I rav'd and grew more fierce and wilde
              At every word,
  Me thoughts I heard one calling, *Childe*:   *marvellous*
           And I reply'd, *My Lord*.   *climax*

The Call

Come, my Way, my Truth, my Life: *Lyric*
Such a Way, as gives us breath:
Such a Truth, as ends all strife:
And such a Life, as killeth death.

Come, my Light, my Feast, my Strength:
Such a Light, as shows a feast:
Such a Feast, as mends in length:
Such a Strength, as makes his guest.

Come, my Joy, my Love, my Heart:
Such a Joy, as none can move:
Such a Love, as none can part:
Such a Heart, as joyes in love.

Clasping of Hands

Lord, thou art mine, and I am thine,
If mine I am : and thine much more,
Then I or ought, or can be mine.
Yet to be thine, doth me restore ;
So that again I now am mine,
And with advantage mine the more.
Since this being mine, brings with it thine,
And thou with me dost thee restore.
    If I without thee would be mine,
    I neither should be mine nor thine.

Lord, I am thine, and thou art mine :
So mine thou art, that something more
I may presume thee mine, then thine.
For thou didst suffer to restore
Not thee, but me, and to be mine :
And with advantage mine the more,
Since thou in death wast none of thine,
Yet then as mine didst me restore.
    O be mine still ! still make me thine !
    Or rather make no Thine and Mine !

The Pulley

notice depth of pacing.

metaphysical conceit

When God at first made man,
Having a glasse of blessings standing by ;
Let us (said he) poure on him all we can :
Let the worlds riches, which dispersed lie,
    Contract into a span.

So strength first made a way ;
Then beautie flow'd, then wisdome, honour, pleasure :
When almost all was out, God made a stay,
Perceiving that alone of all his treasure
    Rest in the bottome lay.

For if I should (said he)
Bestow this jewell also on my creature,
He would adore my gifts in stead of me,
And rest in Nature, not the God of Nature.
So both should losers be.

Yet let him keep the rest,
But keep them with repining restlessnesse : *assonance*
Let him be rich and wearie, that at least,
If goodnesse leade him not, yet wearinesse
May tosse him to my breast.

echoes so much

The Priesthood

Blest Order, which in power dost so excell,
That with th' one hand thou liftest to the sky,
And with the other throwest down to hell
In thy just censures ; fain would I draw nigh,
Fain put thee on, exchanging my lay-sword
For that of th' holy word.

But thou art fire, sacred and hallow'd fire ;
And I but earth and clay : should I presume
To wear thy habit, the severe attire
My slender compositions might consume.
I am both foul and brittle ; much unfit
To deal in holy Writ

Yet have I often seen, by cunning hand
And force of fire, what curious things are made
Of wretched earth. Where once I scorn'd to stand,
That earth is fitted by the fire and trade
Of skilfull artists, for the boards of those
Who make the bravest shows.

But since those great ones, be they ne're so great,
Come from the earth, from whence those vessels come;
So that at once both feeder, dish, and meat
Have one beginning and one finall summe:
I do not greatly wonder at the sight,
                    If earth in earth delight.

But th' holy men of God such vessels are,
As serve him up, who all the world commands:
When God vouchsafeth to become our fare,
Their hands conuey him, who conveys their hands.
O what pure things, most pure must those things be,
                    Who bring my God to me!

Wherefore I dare not, I, put forth my hand
To hold the Ark, although it seem to shake
Through th' old sinnes and new doctrines of our land.
Onely, since God doth often vessels make
Of lowly matter for high uses meet,
                    I throw me at his feet.

There will I lie, untill my Maker seek
For some mean stuffe whereon to show his skill:
Then is my time. The distance of the meek
Doth flatter power. Lest good come short of ill
In praising might, the poore do by submission
                    What pride by opposition.

The Search

Whither, O, whither art thou fled,
                    My Lord, My Love?
My searches are my daily bread;
                    Yet never prove.

My knees pierce th' earth, mine eies the skie;
           And yet the sphere
And centre both to me denie
             That thou art there.

Yet can I mark how herbs below
           Grow green and gay,
As if to meet thee they did know,
            While I decay.

Yet can I mark how starres above
           Simper and shine,
As having keyes unto thy love,
            While poore I pine.

I sent a sigh to seek thee out,
           Deep drawn in pain,
Wing'd like an arrow: but my scout
            Returns in vain.

I tun'd another (having store)
           Into a grone;
Because the search was dumbe before:
            But all was one.

Lord, dost thou some new fabrick mold
           Which favour winnes,
And keeps thee present, leaving th' old
            Unto their sinnes?

Where is my God? what hidden place
           Conceals thee still?
What covert dare eclipse thy face?
            Is it thy will?

O let not that of any thing;
           Let rather brasse,
Or steel, or mountains be thy ring,
            And I will passe.

Thy will such an intrenching is,
                As passeth thought:
To it all strength, all subtilties
                Are things of nought.

Thy will such a strange distance is,
                As that to it
East and West touch, the poles do kisse,
                And parallels meet.

Since then my grief must be as large,
                As is thy space,
Thy distance from me; see my charge,
                Lord, see my case.

O take these barres, these lengths away;
                Turn, and restore me:
Be not Almightie, let me say,
                Against, but for me.

When thou dost turn, and wilt be neare;
                What edge so keen,
What point so piercing can appeare
                To come between?

For as thy absence doth excell
                All distance known:
So doth thy nearenesse bear the bell,
                Making two one.

Grief

O who will give me tears? Come all ye springs,
Dwell in my head & eyes: come clouds, & rain:
My grief hath need of all the watry things,
That nature hath produc'd. Let ev'ry vein

Suck up a river to supply mine eyes,
My weary weeping eyes too drie for me,
Unlesse they get new conduits, new supplies
To beare them out, and with my state agree.
What are two shallow foords, two little spouts
Of a lesse world? the greater is but small,
A narrow cupboard for my griefs and doubts,
Which want provision in the midst of all.
Verses, ye are too fine a thing, too wise
For my rough sorrows: cease, be dumbe and mute,
Give up your feet and running to mine eyes,
And keep your measures for some lovers lute,
Whose grief allows him musick and a ryme:
For mine excludes both measure, tune, and time.
                              Alas, my God!

The Crosse

What is this strange and uncouth thing?
To make me sigh, and seek, and faint, and die,
Untill I had some place, where I might sing,
        And serve thee; and not onely I,
But all my wealth, and familie might combine
To set thy honour up, as our designe.

        And then when after much delay,
Much wrastling, many a combate, this deare end,
So much desir'd, is giv'n, to take away
        My power to serve thee; to unbend
All my abilities, my designes confound,
And lay my threatnings bleeding on the ground.

        One ague dwelleth in my bones,
Another in my soul (the memorie
What I would do for thee, if once my grones
        Could be allow'd for harmonie)

I am in all a weak disabled thing,
Save in the sight thereof, where strength doth sting.

Besides, things sort not to my will,
Ev'n when my will doth studie thy renown:
Thou turnest th' edge of all things on me still,
Taking me up to throw me down:
So that, ev'n when my hopes seem to be sped,
I am to grief alive, to them as dead.

To have my aim, and yet to be
Further from it then when I bent my bow;
To make my hopes my torture, and the fee
Of all my woes another wo,
Is in the midst of delicates to need,
And ev'n in Paradise to be a weed.

Ah my deare Father, ease my smart!
These contrarieties crush me: these crosse actions
Doe winde a rope about, and cut my heart:
And yet since these thy contradictions
Are properly a crosse felt by thy sonne,
With but foure words, my words, *Thy will be done.*

The Flower

How fresh, O Lord, how sweet and clean
Are thy returns! ev'n as the flowers in spring;
To which, besides their own demean,
The late-past frosts tributes of pleasure bring.
Grief melts away
Like snow in May,
As if there were no such cold thing.

Who would have thought my shrivel'd heart
Could have recover'd greennesse? It was gone
 Quite under ground; as flowers depart
To see their mother-root, when they have blown;
   Where they together
   All the hard weather,
Dead to the world, keep house unknown.

These are thy wonders, Lord of power,
Killing and quickning, bringing down to hell
 And up to heaven in an houre;
Making a chiming of a passing-bell.
   We say amisse,
   This or that is:
Thy word is all, if we could spell.

O that I once past changing were,
Fast in thy Paradise, where no flower can wither!
 Many a spring I shoot up fair,
Offring at heav'n, growing and groning thither:
   Nor doth my flower
   Want a spring-showre,
My sinnes and I joining together:

But while I grow in a straight line,
Still upwards bent, as if heav'n were mine own,
 Thy anger comes, and I decline:
What frost to that? what pole is not the zone,
   Where all things burn,
   When thou dost turn,
And the least frown of thine is shown?

And now in age I bud again,
After so many deaths I live and write;
 I once more smell the dew and rain,
And relish versing: O my onely light,
   It cannot be
   That I am he
On whom thy tempests fell all night.

These are thy wonders, Lord of love,
To make us see we are but flowers that glide:
  Which when we once can finde and prove,
Thou hast a garden for us, where to bide.
        Who would be more,
          Swelling through store,
Forfeit their Paradise by their pride.

Dotage

False glozing pleasures, casks of happinesse,
Foolish night-fires, womens and childrens wishes,
Chases in Arras, guilded emptinesse,
Shadows well mounted, dreams in a career,
Embroider'd lyes, nothing between two dishes;
        These are the pleasures here.

True earnest sorrows, rooted miseries,
Anguish in grain, vexations ripe and blown,
Sure-footed griefs, solid calamities,
Plain demonstrations, evident and cleare,
Fetching their proofs ev'n from the very bone;
        These are the sorrows here.

But oh the folly of distracted men,
Who griefs in earnest, joyes in jest pursue;
Preferring, like brute beasts, a lothsome den
Before a court, ev'n that above so cleare,
Where are no sorrows, but delights more true,
        Then miseries are here!

The Sonne

Let forrain nations of their language boast,
What fine varietie each tongue affords:
I like our language, as our men and coast:
Who cannot dresse it well, want wit, not words.
How neatly doe we give one onely name
To parents issue and the sunnes bright starre!
A sonne is light and fruit; a fruitfull flame
Chasing the fathers dimnesse, carri'd farre
From the first man in th' East, to fresh and new
Western discov'ries of posteritie.
So in one word our Lords humilitie
We turn upon him in a sense most true:
   For what Christ once in humblenesse began,
   We him in glorie call, *The Sonne of Man.*

A True Hymne

My joy, my life, my crown!
My heart was meaning all the day,
   Somewhat it fain would say:
And still it runneth mutt'ring up and down
With onely this, *My joy, my life, my crown.*

   Yet slight not these few words:
If truly said, they may take part
   Among the best in art.
The finenesse which a hymne or psalme affords,
Is, when the soul unto the lines accords.

   He who craves all the minde,
And all the soul, and strength, and time,
   If the words onely ryme,
Justly complains, that somewhat is behinde
To make his verse, or write a hymne in kinde.

Whereas if th' heart be moved,
Although the verse be somewhat scant,
God doth supplie the want.
As when th' heart sayes (sighing to be approved)
O, *could I love!* and stops: God writeth, *Loved.*

The Answer

My comforts drop and melt away like snow:
I shake my head, and all the thoughts and ends,
Which my fierce youth did bandie, fall and flow
Like leaves about me; or like summer friends,
Flyes of estates and sunne-shine. But to all,
Who think me eager, hot, and undertaking,
But in my prosecutions slack and small;
As a young exhalation, newly waking,
Scorns his first bed of dirt, and means the sky;
But cooling by the way, grows pursie and slow,
And setling to a cloud, doth live and die
In that dark state of tears: to all, that so
Show me, and set me, I have one reply,
Which they that know the rest, know more then I.

A Dialogue-Antheme

Christian.   Death.

Chr.   Alas, poore Death, where is thy glorie?
Where is thy famous force, thy ancient sting?
Dea.   *Alas poore mortall, void of storie,*
Go spell and reade how I have kill'd thy King.
Chr.   Poore death! and who was hurt thereby?
Thy curse being laid on him, makes thee accurst.
Dea.   *Let losers talk: yet thou shalt die;*
These arms shall crush thee.   Chr. Spare not, do thy worst.
I shall be one day better then before:
Thou so much worse, that thou shalt be no more.

78

Bitter-sweet

(handwritten margin note: perfect lyric privilege of love)

Ah my deare angrie Lord,
Since thou dost love, yet strike;
Cast down, yet help afford;
Sure I will do the like.
I will complain, yet praise;
I will bewail, approve:
And all my sowre-sweet dayes
I will lament, and love.

The Glance

When first thy sweet and gracious eye
Vouchsaf'd ev'n in the midst of youth and night
To look upon me, who before did lie
    Weltring in sinne;
I felt a sugred strange delight,
Passing all cordials made by any art,
Bedew, embalme, and overrunne my heart,
    And take it in.

Since that time many a bitter storm
My soul hath felt, ev'n able to destroy,
Had the malicious and ill-meaning harm
    His swing and sway:
But still thy sweet originall joy
Sprung from thine eye, did work within my soul,
And surging griefs, when they grew bold, controll,
    And got the day.

If thy first glance so powerfull be,
A mirth but open'd and seal'd up again;
What wonders shall we feel, when we shall see
    Thy full-ey'd love!

When thou shalt look us out of pain,
And one aspect of thine spend in delight
More then a thousand sunnes disburse in light,
    In heav'n above.

Aaron

    Holinesse on the head,
Light and perfections on the breast,
Harmonious bells below, raising the dead
To leade them unto life and rest.
    Thus are true Aarons drest.

    Profanenesse in my head,
Defects and darknesse in my breast,
A noise of passions ringing me for dead
Unto a place where is no rest,
    Poore priest thus am I drest.

    Onely another head
I have, another heart and breast,
Another musick, making live not dead,
Without whom I could have no rest :
    In him I am well drest.

    Christ is my onely head,
My alone onely heart and breast,
My onely musick, striking me ev'n dead ;
That to the old man I may rest,
    And be in him new drest.

    So holy in my head,
Perfect and light in my deare breast,
My doctrine tun'd by Christ, (who is not dead,
But lives in me while I do rest)
    Come people ; Aaron's drest.

The Odour

2 Cor. 11.

How sweetly doth *My Master* sound ! *My Master!*
        As Amber-greese leaves a rich sent
                Unto the taster:
        So do these words a sweet content,
An orientall fragrancie, *My Master*.

With these all day I do perfume my minde,
        My minde ev'n thrust into them both:
                That I might finde
        What cordials make this curious broth,
This broth of smells, that feeds and fats my minde.

My Master, shall I speak? O that to thee
        My servant were a little so,
                As flesh may be;
        That these two words might creep & grow
To some degree of spicinesse to thee !

Then should the Pomander, which was before
        A speaking sweet, mend by reflection,
                And tell me more:
        For pardon of my imperfection
Would warm and work it sweeter then before.

For when *My Master*, which alone is sweet,
        And ev'n in my unworthinesse pleasing,
                Shall call and meet,
        My servant, as thee not displeasing,
That call is but the breathing of the sweet.

This breathing would with gains by sweetning me
        (As sweet things traffick when they meet)
                Return to thee.
        And so this new commerce and sweet
Should all my life employ, and busie me.

The Foil

If we could see below
The sphere of vertue, and each shining grace
As plainly as that above doth show;
This were the better skie, the brighter place.

God hath made starres the foil
To set off vertues; griefs to set off sinning:
Yet in this wretched world we toil,
As if grief were not foul, nor vertue winning.

The Forerunners

The harbingers are come. See, see their mark;
White is their colour, and behold my head.
But must they have my brain? must they dispark
Those sparkling notions, which therein were bred?
Must dulnesse turn me to a clod?
Yet have they left me, *Thou art still my God.*

Good men ye be, to leave me my best room,
Ev'n all my heart, and what is lodged there:
I passe not, I, what of the rest become,
So *Thou art still my God,* be out of fear.
He will be pleased with that dittie;
And if I please him, I write fine and wittie.

Farewell sweet phrases, lovely metaphors.
But will ye leave me thus? when ye before
Of stews and brothels onely knew the doores,
Then did I wash you with my tears, and more,
Brought you to Church well drest and clad:
My God must have my best, ev'n all I had.

Louely enchanting language, sugar-cane,
Hony of roses, whither wilt thou flie?
Hath some fond lover tic'd thee to thy bane?
And wilt thou leave the Church, and love a stie?
      Fie, thou wilt soil thy broider'd coat,
And hurt thy self, and him that sings the note.

Let foolish lovers, if they will love dung,
With canvas, not with arras clothe their shame:
Let follie speak in her own native tongue.
True beautie dwells on high: ours is a flame
      But borrow'd thence to light us thither.
Beautie and beauteous words should go together.

Yet if you go, I passe not; take your way:
For, *Thou art still my God*, is all that ye
Perhaps with more embellishment can say,
Go birds of spring: let winter have his fee,
      Let a bleak palenesse chalk the doore,
So all within be livelier then before.

The Rose

Presse me not to take more pleasure
      In this world of sugred lies,
And to use a larger measure
      Then my strict, yet welcome size.

First, there is no pleasure here:
      Colour'd griefs indeed there are,
Blushing woes, that look as cleare
      As if they could beautie spare.

Or if such deceits there be,
      Such delights I meant to say;
There are no such things to me,
      Who have pass'd my right away.

But I will not much oppose
      Unto what you now advise:
Onely take this gentle rose,
      And therein my answer lies.

What is fairer then a rose?
      What is sweeter? yet it purgeth
Purgings enmitie disclose,
      Enmitie forbearance urgeth.

If then all that worldlings prize
      Be contracted to a rose;
Sweetly there indeed it lies,
      But it biteth in the close.

So this flower doth judge and sentence
      Worldly joyes to be a scourge:
For they all produce repentance,
      And repentance is a purge.

But I health, not physick choose:
      Onely though I you oppose,
Say that fairly I refuse,
      For my answer is a rose.

Discipline

Throw away thy rod,
Throw away thy wrath:
      O my God,
Take the gentle path.

utter simplicity of writing but true poetry.

For my hearts desire
Unto thine is bent:
            I aspire
To a full consent.

Not a word or look
I affect to own,
            But by book,
And thy book alone.

Though I fail, I weep:
Though I halt in pace,
            Yet I creep
To the throne of grace.

Then let wrath remove;
Love will do the deed:
            For with love
Stonie hearts will bleed

Love is swift of foot;
Love's a man of warre,
            And can shoot,
And can hit from farre.

Who can scape his bow?
That which wrought on thee,
            Brought thee low,
Needs must work on me.

Throw away thy rod;
Though man frailties hath,
            Thou art God:
Throw away thy wrath.

The Banquet

Welcome sweet and sacred cheer,
          Welcome deare:
With me, in me, live and dwell:
For thy neatnesse passeth sight,
          Thy delight
Passeth tongue to taste or tell.

O what sweetnesse from the bowl
          Fills my soul,
Such as is, and makes divine!
Is some starre (fled from the sphere)
          Melted there,
As we sugar melt in wine?

Or hath sweetnesse in the bread
          Made a head
To subdue the smell of sinne;
Flowers, and gummes, and powders giving
          All their living,
Lest the enemie should winne?

Doubtlesse, neither starre nor flower
          Hath the power
Such a sweetnesse to impart:
Onely God, who gives perfumes,
          Flesh assumes,
And with it perfumes my heart.

But as Pomanders and wood
          Still are good,
Yet being bruis'd are better sented:
God, to show how farre his love
          Could improve,
Here, as broken, is presented.

When I had forgot my birth,
                    And on earth
In delights of earth was drown'd;
God took bloud, and needs would be
                    Spilt with me,
And so found me on the ground.

Having rais'd me to look up,
                    In a cup
Sweetly he doth meet my taste.
But I still being low and short,
                    Farre from court,
Wine becomes a wing at last.

For with it alone I flie
                    To the skie:
Where I wipe mine eyes, and see
What I seek, for what I sue;
                    Him I view,
Who hath done so much for me.

Let the wonder of this pitie
                    Be my dittie,
And take up my lines and life:
Hearken under pain of death,
                    Hands and breath;
Strive in this, and love the strife.

The Posie

Let wits contest,
And with their words and posies windows fill:
            Lesse then the least
Of all thy mercies, is my posie still.

This on my ring,
This by my picture, in my book I write:
Whether I sing,
Or say, or dictate, this is my delight.

Invention rest,
Comparisons go play, wit use thy will:
Lesse then the least
Of all Gods mercies, is my posie still.

The Elixer

Teach me, my God and King,
In all things thee to see,
And what I do in any thing,
To do it as for thee:

Not rudely, as a beast,
To runne into an action;
But still to make thee prepossest,
And give it his perfection.

A man that looks on glasse,
On it may stay his eye;
Or if he pleaseth, through it passe,
And then the heav'n espie.

All may of thee partake:
Nothing can be so mean,
Which with his tincture (for thy sake)
Will not grow bright and clean.

A servant with this clause
Makes drudgerie divine:
Who sweeps a room, as for thy laws,
Makes that and th' action fine.

This is the famous stone
That turneth all to gold:
For that which God doth touch and own
Cannot for lesse be told.

A Wreath

A wreathed garland of deserved praise,
Of praise deserved, unto thee I give,
I give to thee, who knowest all my wayes,
My crooked winding wayes, wherein I live,
Wherein I die, not live: for life is straight,
Straight as a line, and ever tends to thee,
To thee, who art more farre above deceit,
Then deceit seems above simplicitie.
Give me simplicitie, that I may live,
So live and like, that I may know thy wayes,
Know them and practise them: then shall I give
For this poore wreath, give thee a crown of praise.

Judgement

Almightie Judge, how shall poore wretches brook
Thy dreadfull look,
Able a heart of iron to appall,
When thou shalt call
For ev'ry mans peculiar book?

What others mean to do, I know not well;
Yet I heare tell,
That some will turn thee to some leaves therein
So void of sinne,
That they in merit shall excell.

89

But I resolve, when thou shalt call for mine,
        That to decline,
And thrust a Testament into thy hand:
        Let that be scann'd.
    There thou shalt finde my faults are thine.

Heaven

O who will show me those delights on high?
        Echo.   *I.*
Thou Echo, thou art mortall, all men know.
        Echo.   *No.*
Wert thou not born among the trees and leaves?
        Echo.   *Leaves.*
And are there any leaves, that still abide?
        Echo.   *Bide.*
What leaves are they? impart the matter wholly.
        Echo.   *Holy.*
Are holy leaves the Echo then of blisse?
        Echo.   *Yes.*
Then tell me, what is that supreme delight?
        Echo.   *Light.*
Light to the minde: what shall the will enjoy?
        Echo.   *Joy.*
But are there cares and businesse with the pleasure?
        Echo.   *Leisure.*
Light, joy, and leisure; but shall they persever?
        Echo.   *Ever.*

'peasonifying love
metaphor heis in
sitting down to feast

Love

Love bade me welcome: yet my soul drew back,
    Guiltie of dust and sinne.
But quick-ey'd Love, observing me grow slack
    From my first entrance in,
Drew nearer to me, sweetly questioning,
    If I lack'd any thing.

A guest, I answer'd, worthy to be here:
    Love said, you shall be he.
I the unkinde, ungratefull? Ah my deare,
    I cannot look on thee.
Love took my hand, and smiling did reply,
    Who made the eyes but I?

Truth Lord, but I have marr'd them: let my shame
    Go where it doth deserve.
And know you not, sayes Love, who bore the blame?
    My deare, then I will serve.
You must sit down, sayes Love, and taste my meat:
    So I did sit and eat.

*dialogue
they didn't
use livered
coras*

From Walton's *Life of Mr. George Herbert*

My God, where is that ancient heat towards thee
    Wherewith whole showls of Martyrs once did burn,
    Besides their other flames? Doth Poetry
Wear Venus Livery? only serve her turn?
Why are not Sonnets made of thee? and layes
    Upon thine Altar burnt? Cannot thy love
    Heighten a spirit to sound out thy praise
As well as any she? Cannot thy Dove
Out-strip their Cupid easily in flight?
    Or, since thy ways are deep, and still the same,
    Will not a verse run smooth that bears thy name!

Why doth that power, which by thy power and might
    Each breast does feel, no braver fuel choose
    Than that, which one day, Worms may chance refuse?
Sure Lord, there is enough in thee to dry
    Oceans of Ink; for, as the Deluge did
    Cover the Earth, so doth thy Majesty:
Each cloud distils thy praise, and doth forbid
Poets to turn it to another use.
    Roses and Lillies speak thee; and to make
    A pair of Cheeks of them, is thy abuse.
Why should I Womens eyes for Chrystal take?
Such poor invention burns in their low mind
    Whose fire is wild, and doth not upward go
    To praise, and, on thee Lord, some Ink bestow.
Open the bones, and you shall nothing find
    In the best face but filth; when Lord, in thee
    The beauty lies in the discovery.

Index of First Lines